Make Out

Make Out

60 romantic recipes for gettin' it on

Tonia George

MQP

Published by **MQ Publications Limited**
12 The Ivories, 6–8 Northampton Street
London N1 2HY
Tel: 44 (0)20 7359 2244
Fax: 44 (0)20 7359 1616
email: mail@mqpublications.com
website: www.mqpublications.com

Design and illustration: Jo Hill
Photography: Janine Hosegood
Home Economy: Tonia George

ISBN: 1-84072-794-2

1 3 5 7 9 0 8 6 4 2

Printed and bound in France by *Partenaires-Livres*® (JL)

Introduction

Food isn't the only way to a man's heart—it's the way to any lover's heart! Whether it's finger-licking bites to tempt the appetite and clear the path for flirtatious banter, or naughty nibbles to indulge yourselves in between the sheets, you're sure to find the ideal aphrodisiac among these pages.

Are you looking for the perfect romantic meal to seduce your lover, or a few lovingly prepared morsels to share from a single plate? There's nothing like fighting over the last oyster drenched in Tabasco and lemon juice to raise your passions and get your blood pumping!

Or, if you've got a sweet tooth, how about indulging your wicked side with one of the lusciously lovely or truly intoxicating desserts? Feed your lover tiny mouthfuls of strawberries coated in hazelnut caramel, or let chocolate fondue dribble down your chin and let your partner lick it off. Alternatively, just submerge yourself in sweet, creamy white and dark chocolate cheesecake with raspberries, and worry about the love part later!

Get in tune with your lover through their taste buds and let the food do the hard work. You just reap the benefits ...

1

Flirtatious Foreplay
Love potions & tempting teasers

Mango & Lime Caipirinha

This Brazilian drink is fantastic on its own or drunk with spicy food. It goes especially well with Thai flavours. If you can't find cachaça—the Brazilian spirit made from sugar-cane juice—you can use vodka instead.

MAKES 2

2 limes, cut into small wedges
1 tbsp turbinado sugar
2½ tbsp cachaça
½ cup/120ml mango juice
Handful of ice

1 Place the limes in a pitcher with the sugar and carefully crush with the end of a rolling pin until most of the juice has been extracted.

2 Pour the cachaça and mango juice over the limes. Top up with ice and serve.

> **Cook's Tip**
>
> Turbinado sugar contains molasses, which gives this fabulous tipple a rich flavor and warm amber colour.

Little Devil

A tipple to bring out your wicked side!

MAKES 2

Handful of ice
2 tbsp lemon juice
2 tbsp Cointreau
4 tbsp dark rum
1½ tbsp gin

1 Put the ice in the cocktail shaker and pour over the lemon juice, Cointreau, rum, and gin.

2 Holding the cocktail shaker in a cloth, shake the ingredients together until well mixed and ice cold. Pour into shot glasses and serve immediately.

White Peach Bellini

If you can find white peaches for this cocktail, they give a delightfully elegant result—but regular peaches will do just as well if white ones aren't available.

MAKES 2

2 tbsp peach schnapps
2 tbsp brandy
1 very ripe white peach, peeled
  and pitted
1 cup/240ml chilled Asti Spumante

1 Pour the peach schnapps and brandy into a blender, add the peach, and blend until very smooth.

2 Pour the mixture into two glasses and top up with champagne. Stir, then drink.

> **Cook's Tip**
>
> Asti spumante—a sweet Italian wine—is the traditional choice for this classic cocktail, but any sparkling wine will do.

Spanish Seranade

If you're not up for singing to your lover, try this number out for size instead.

MAKES 2

6 tbsp dry sherry
6 tbsp Grand Marnier
Juice of 1 lemon juice
Juice of 2 oranges
Lightly crushed ice

1 Mix together the sherry, Grand Marnier, and lemon and orange juices.

2 Fill two tall glasses with crushed ice and pour over the cocktail. If liked, decorate with strips of citrus peel.

Cosmopolitan

This is the ultimate cocktail for sexy, sassy girls. Perfect at any time of the day, but best saved for after dark. If you're off on a man-hunt, it's the perfect way to start the evening ...

MAKES 2

1 tbsp lime cordial
3 tbsp citron vodka
1 tbsp triple sec or Cointreau
1 cup/240ml cranberry juice
2 handfuls of ice

1 Pour the lime cordial, vodka, triple sec or Cointreau, and cranberry juice into a cocktail shaker.

2 Add the ice, shake well, and strain into two chilled cocktail glasses.

Champagne Laced
with Raspberries

Here's something tempting to get the evening off with a real swing. Luscious, plump red raspberries look divine but the white ones—which are available throughout late summer—add a wonderfully sophisticated edge.

MAKES 2 (WITH A TOP UP)

6 red or white raspberries
2 tbsp white rum
1½ cups/350ml bottle of chilled champagne
Dash of angostura bitters

1 Place a few raspberries in the bottom of each champagne flute and divide the rum between them.

2 Top up with champagne and add a dash of angostura to each flute. As you drink, top up with the extra champagne.

Silk Stocking

This creamy, dreamy cocktail is more of an after-dinner affair and makes a perfect substitute for dessert. Enjoy it whilst lounging in front of a roaring fire.

MAKES 2

3 tbsp white tequila
4 tbsp light cream
3 tbsp crème de cacao or Malibu
1 tbsp grenadine
2 handfuls ice

1 Pour the tequila, cream, crème de cacao or malibu, and grenadine into a blender, then add the ice. Blend well, then pour the mixture into two short glasses and serve immediately.

Cook's Tip

Check the manufacturer's instructions on your blender to ensure that it is suitable for blending ice.

Strawberry Sweethearts

Win your lover's heart with this ice-cold, frothy milkshake.

MAKES 2

2 cups/200g strawberries, hulled
1 ripe banana, peeled
1 tbsp sugar
1¼ cups/280ml milk
2 scoops vanilla ice cream

1 Pick out a small strawberry and cut in half to make two hearts. Set aside.

2 Put the remaining strawberries in a blender with the banana, sugar, milk, and ice cream. Blend until thick and frothy and pour into two stemmed glasses. Decorate with the strawberry hearts and serve immediately.

Up-all-night Espressatini

Just one glass of this turbo-charged cocktail will have you wide awake and ready for action. The mouth-watering mix of vodka and caffeine is guaranteed to get you going, and keep you going ... all night!

MAKES 2

2 tbsp hot, strong, freshly made espresso
2 tsp sugar
3 tbsp vodka
1 tbsp Kahlua or Tia Maria
Handful of ice

1 While the espresso is still hot, add the sugar and stir until dissolved.

2 Pour the coffee into a cocktail shaker, then add the vodka, Kahlua or Tia Maria, and ice and shake well. Strain into two chilled glasses and serve immediately.

Passionate Embrace

To vary the flavors of this lip-smacking refresher, try different juices such as guava or mango.

MAKES 2

Caster sugar, for frosting
2 sugar lumps
2 tbsp brandy
90ml/3fl oz chilled passion fruit juice
Chilled sparkling dry white wine

1 Dip the rims of two champagne flutes first in cold water and then in a little caster sugar to frost them. Set aside until ready to serve.

2 If using the sugar lumps, drop them into the glasses. Pour in the brandy, then add the passion fruit juice.

3 Top up with the chilled sparkling wine and serve immediately.

Oysters with Shallot & Red Wine Vinaigrette

Fresh oysters have been enjoyed as an aphrodisiac for centuries and even today still seem to hold the same potent power. The shells are simple to open once you know how. The first one may take a while but after that you'll soon get the hang of it.

MAKES 6

½ dozen oysters
1 shallot, finely chopped
4 tbsp red wine vinegar

> **Cook's Tip**
>
> If you don't have an oyster knife, don't rush out and buy one specially. You can use a sturdy flat-headed screwdriver instead—it will work just as well.

1 Before opening the oysters, wrap your hand in a dishtowel to protect it, then hold one of the oysters in the wrapped hand, flat side up.

2 Slide an oyster knife into the hinge end of the oyster and move it back and forth gently, pressing it further in to prize the shell open.

3 Once the shell releases, scrape a knife across the flat side of the shell to release the oyster. Discard the top shell and leave the oyster in the bottom half. Repeat with the remaining oysters.

4 Mix together the shallot with the red wine vinegar and transfer to a small bowl. To eat take a teaspoonful of vinaigrette and drizzle it over the oyster, then simply slip the oyster into your mouth.

Sexy Sushi Hand Rolls

Sushi is surprisingly easy to make at home and tastes wonderful—perfect for slipping into your mouth between sips of a pre-dinner drink. Hand rolls are the easiest to make because you don't need to roll the sushi in a bamboo mat.

MAKES 5

½ cup/125g short grain rice
½ tsp sugar
1 tbsp rice wine vinegar
½ tbsp mirin
½ tsp wasabi
1 tbsp mayonnaise
6oz/175g crab meat (fresh or canned)
½ avocado, stoned, flesh scooped out
   with a large spoon
5 sheets nori seaweed, trimmed to
   10cm squares
5 sprigs watercress or arugula

1 To make the sticky rice, place the rice in a small pan with 1 cup/240ml water. Cover and simmer over a very low heat for 8 minutes, or until the liquid has been absorbed. Turn off the heat and leave the rice to steam. Take off the heat and cool to room temperature, then stir in the sugar, rice wine vinegar, and mirin.

2 To make the filling, mix together the wasabi, mayonnaise, and crab. Slice the avocado into five long slices.

3 Spread one-fifth of the rice diagonally down the center of the nori sheet. Lay a slice of avocado across this and then spoon over one-fifth of the crab mixture and top with a sprig of watercress or arugula. Fold into a cone, using a few grains of the sticky rice to stick the edges together. Repeat with the remaining nori sheets and filling and serve.

Roasted Asparagus Tips
with Lemon Aioli

Nothing beats this finger-licking temptation to dip and enjoy whilst getting to know each other that little bit better. The creamy, zesty aioli helps to stimulate all your senses.

SERVES 2

4oz/115g asparagus tips
1 tbsp olive oil
4 slices Serrano ham, cut into ¾in/2cm
  wide strips
Lemon aioli
2 tbsp mayonnaise
1 tbsp lemon juice and rind of ½ unwaxed
  lemon
1 small garlic clove, crushed

1 Preheat the oven to 400°F/200°C/ Gas 6. Place the asparagus on a baking tray and drizzle with the oil. Roast for 6–8 minutes depending on the thickness of the asparagus—it should be just tender. Remove from the oven and leave to cool slightly.

2 Mix together the mayonnaise, lemon juice and rind, and crushed garlic, and transfer to a small serving bowl. Wrap the Serrano ham casually around the asparagus and serve with the dip.

Morsels of Halloumi
Drizzled with Mint & Chili Oil

These salty little bites are wonderfully moreish. You can play around with the flavor of the oil if you fancy a change by using different herbs. Try fresh basil, oregano or thyme—they all taste great.

SERVES 2

¼ tsp chili flakes
½ tbsp finely chopped fresh mint
2 tbsp extra virgin olive oil
1 (9oz/250g) packet halloumi cheese, drained and cut into ¾in/2 cm cubes

1 In a small bowl, mix together the chili flakes, fresh mint, and olive oil.

2 Heat a heavy non-stick skillet over a high heat and fry the halloumi for about 3 minutes until nicely golden, turning it with tongs so that it cooks on all sides. Transfer to a plate and drizzle with the flavored oil. Serve.

Honey-roasted Nuts
with Fragrant Fennel Seeds

These sweet and sticky nuts are the perfect thing to nibble on while you sip the cocktail of your choice. Choose something chilled and sophisticated, such as a Cosmopolitan or a Mango and Lime Caipirinha.

SERVES 2

1½ cups/250g mixed nuts, such as filberts, cashews, almonds, and pecan nuts
1 tsp fennel seeds
3 tbsp clear honey
2 tbsp dark soy sauce
Finely grated rind of ½ orange

1 Place the nuts and fennel seeds in a dry frying pan and toast over a medium heat for 3–4 minutes, tossing occasionally until golden brown all over.

2 Drizzle the honey over the nuts and seeds and toss over the heat for 1 minute, or until the nuts are well coated. Add the soy sauce and orange rind and cook for 30 seconds until the liquid evaporates.

3 Tip the nuts on to a sheet of waxed paper and spread out so that they form small clusters. Leave to cool before serving with drinks.

Mini-blinis with Smoked Salmon & Beet Caviar

These fabulous bites were just made to be eaten with shots of ice cold, high-quality vodka, but a small glass of bubbly will do just as well. You can use other types of smoked fish if you prefer.

MAKES 16

2 tbsp crème fraîche
1 tsp grated horseradish
16 cocktail blinis, or discs of
  pumpernickel bread
4oz/115g smoked salmon trimmings,
  cut into strips
1 small cooked beet, very finely
  chopped

1 Mix together the crème fraîche and horseradish. Warm the blinis or pumpernickel in an oven preheated to 400°F/200°C/Gas 6 or in a microwave, according to the packet instructions.

2 Top each blini or pumpernickel disc with a small amount of the crème fraîche mixture, making sure they are placed on a flat surface so that the mixture doesn't slide off. Top this with a strip of smoked salmon and finally a small amount of finely chopped beet. Serve immediately.

2

Between the Sheets

Breakfast in bed and late-night nibbles

Soft Boiled Duck Eggs with Asparagus and Chorizo Dippers

Pure-white duck eggs are lovely looking and have beautiful rich yolks, making them perfect for dipping. Chorizo and asparagus dipped in a soft cooked egg are two of the closest things to heaven— you need to try it to believe it.

SERVES 2

2 large free-range duck eggs
7oz/200g asparagus, trimmed
4oz/115g chorizo sausage, sliced

Cook's Tip

If you can't get hold of duck eggs, use white hen's eggs instead. They're slightly larger than duck eggs, so you'll need to cook them for 1 minute more to ensure a firm white and runny yolk.

---

1 Place the eggs in a pan of cold water over a high heat and bring to the boil. Once boiling, reduce the heat to low and simmer gently for 3 minutes. Drain.

2 Meanwhile, gently simmer the asparagus in a pan of salted boiling water for 3 minutes, and then drain.

3 Heat a frying pan over a medium heat, then add the chorizo and dry-fry for about 30 seconds on each side until crispy.

4 Serve the boiled eggs in eggcups with the tops sliced off, and arrange the chorizo and asparagus on a plate for dipping into the soft yolk.

Avocado on Toast

with Bacon & Roasted Tomatoes

Smooth, creamy, buttery avocado spread on toast with crisp, salty bacon and sweet roasted tomatoes is the ultimate bedtime treat. Seek out a creamily ripe avocado with a good flavor to make this sumptuous snack.

SERVES 2

2 plum tomatoes, cut into 3 slices
  lengthways
8 strips fatty bacon
1 avocado, pitted and peeled
4 slices ciabatta
Salt and freshly ground black pepper

1 Preheat the oven to 325°F/160°C/Gas 3. Place the tomatoes on a baking sheet, cut side up, and roast for 45 minutes.

2 When they are nearly cooked, broil or fry the bacon until crispy and drain on kitchen paper. Keep warm.

3 Place the avocado in a bowl and mash it, seasoning with salt and pepper. Toast the ciabatta and spread with the avocado. Top with the bacon and roast tomatoes and serve piping hot.

Creamy Scrambled Eggs
on Focaccia with Truffle Oil

Scrambled eggs cooked slowly with lots of love need no cream to be rich and creamy. Here, they are drizzled with truffle oil, the smell of which is said to be a natural aphrodisiac.

SERVES 2

5 free-range eggs, beaten
2 tbsp/30g butter, plus extra to butter
½ small focaccia or ciabatta, split in half
2 tsp truffle oil
Salt and freshly ground black pepper

1 Beat the eggs together with a little salt and freshly ground black pepper. Melt half the butter in a heavy pan over a very low heat and add the eggs. Cook slowly for 6–8 minutes, stirring constantly until they start to thicken.

2 Once the eggs start to thicken, stir constantly, scraping the spoon across the bottom of the pan to prevent the eggs sticking. Remove from the heat when the eggs are just set.

3 Meanwhile toast the focaccia or ciabatta, and spread with butter. Pile the eggs on to the toast and drizzle with the truffle oil. Serve immediately.

Smoked Salmon & Basil Cream Cheese Bagels

Smoked salmon and cream cheese bagels are always the ultimate treat—whether they're for breakfast, brunch, or a late night snack. Adding fresh basil gives them a lovely peppery, fragrant taste.

SERVES 2

½ cup/125g cream cheese
8 basil leaves, finely chopped
2 bagels, split in half
4 slices smoked salmon
Freshly ground black pepper

1 In a small bowl beat together the cream cheese and basil.

2 Spread the mixture over each bagel half and fold two slices of smoked salmon on top of each one. Add a grinding of fresh black pepper and serve.

French Toast with Passion Fruit & Vanilla Syrup

This fruity little number is one of the sexiest, most luscious breakfast dishes ever. It just has to be enjoyed in bed—ideally off one plate.

SERVES 2

1 free-range egg, beaten
1 tbsp heavy cream
4 slices challah or white bread, sliced ¾in/2cm thick
3 tbsp oil
For the syrup
3 large passion fruit, halved
1 vanilla bean, split lengthwise
2 tbsp water
1 tbsp sugar

1 To make the syrup, scoop the passion fruit pulp into a small pan and add the vanilla bean, water, and sugar. Place over a low heat and simmer for 5 minutes, or until syrupy, then leave to cool slightly.

2 Meanwhile, place the egg in a bowl and beat with the cream. Dip in the bread into the mixture so each slice is covered completely on both sides.

3 Heat the oil in a skillet over a medium heat, add the eggy bread, and fry for 1–2 minutes on each side, or until lightly golden. Serve immediately with the syrup drizzled over.

Toasted Brioche Topped
with Poached Apricots

Rise early and get some fresh buttery
brioche from the bakery to make this
breakfast a special one. If you can't find
brioche buns, you can use thick slices
of brioche instead.

SERVES 2

4 apricots, halved and pitted
1 cup/240ml orange juice
1 cinnamon stick
Pinch freshly grated nutmeg
2 brioche buns, halved horizontally
4 tbsp crème fraîche
1 tbsp/10g toasted filberts, chopped

1 Place the apricots snugly in a small
pan, pour over the orange juice and
sprinkle with the spices. Heat gently and
simmer for 7–10 minutes, until softened,
turning occasionally so that they cook
evenly. (The time needed will depend on
the ripeness of the fruit.)

2 Using a slotted spoon, remove the
apricots from the juice and set aside. Boil
the liquid in the pan for 3–4 minutes, or
until thickened and syrupy.

3 Meanwhile, toast the brioche on the
cut sides only, under the broiler or on a
griddle pan until lightly golden.

4 Spread the bottom slices of brioche
with the crème fraîche. Spoon the
apricots on top and scatter with the
toasted nuts. Cover with the brioche tops,
and serve immediately.

Blueberry Pancakes with Whipped Butter & Maple Syrup

Freshly made light and fluffy pancakes with pockets of bursting blueberries, smothered in whipped butter and maple syrup make a perfect lover's feast. For the best flavor, look out for authentic, good-quality maple syrup.

SERVES 2

Oil, for greasing
1¼ cups/145g all-purpose flour
Pinch salt
1 tbsp superfine sugar
3 tsp baking powder
1 cup/125g blueberries
1 cup/240ml buttermilk
2 eggs, beaten
3 tbsp/45g melted butter
Maple syrup, to serve
For the whipped butter
3 tbsp/45g butter
3 tbsp milk

1 To make the whipped butter, place the butter in a small bowl. Using an electric hand beater, beat the butter until fluffy, then gradually beat in the milk.

2 Heat a flat griddle or non-stick skillet over a very low heat and wipe with a piece of kitchen paper dabbed in oil. Combine the flour, salt, sugar, and blueberries in a mixing bowl.

3 In a pitcher, beat together the buttermilk, eggs, and melted butter, then pour the mixture into the dry ingredients and mix well to combine.

4 Ladle 3 tbsp of the batter on to the griddle or pan and cook for 2–3 minutes, or until dry around the edges and bubbling on top. Turn and cook for another 1–2 minutes on the other side until cooked through. Cook the remaining batter in the same way, then serve with the whipped butter and maple syrup.

Raisin Toast with Ricotta, Lime, Honey & Strawberries

This is an incredibly quick breakfast to throw together, but it looks impressive and tastes sublime. Other summer fruits are great too—try slices of ripe nectarine, or juicy pitted cherries.

SERVES 2

4 slices raisin or fruit bread
½ cup/125g ricotta cheese
Finely grated rind of 1 lime
1 tbsp clear honey
1 cup/100g strawberries, hulled
  and quartered

1 Toast the raisin bread under the broiler or in the toaster. Meanwhile, mix together the ricotta cheese and lime rind in a small bowl until well-blended.

2 Whilst the toast is hot, spread with the ricotta cheese mixture and drizzle with honey. Scatter over the strawberries and serve immediately.

Sweet Sticky Plum & Almond Pastries

Nothing could be more seductive or indulgent than these oozingly sweet pastries. Enjoy them as a naughty breakfast with piping hot coffee, or an even naughtier midnight snack.

MAKES 6

13oz/375g ready-rolled puff pastry, thawed if frozen
½ cup/175g natural marzipan, cubed
5 tbsp heavy cream
4 peaches or plums, halved, pitted, and thinly sliced
1oz/25g slivered almonds
Confectioner's sugar, for dusting

1 Preheat the oven to 400°F/200°C/ Gas 6. Cut the pastry into six rectangles measuring 4 × 2¾in/10 × 7cm.

2 Place the marzipan and cream in a food processor and process until smooth. Spoon the mixture across the center of the pastries and top with the fruit. Scatter over the slivered almonds and bake for 15–18 minutes, or until lightly golden. Dust with confectioner's sugar before serving.

Chocolate & Cinnamon Croque-monsieur

Here is something for those who love the French classic, but for whom only chocolate will do. Warm, spicy, and oozingly sticky—you might even need a hand with licking those fingers!

SERVES 2

4 slices white bread, crusts removed
1 tbsp/15g butter, softened
2oz/50g bittersweet chocolate,
   coarsely grated
1 tbsp confectioner's sugar
Large pinch ground cinnamon

1 Butter each slice of bread on one side. Place two slices of the buttered bread on a board, butter side down, and scatter with the grated chocolate. Place the second slice on top, buttered side up.

2 Heat a heavy skillet over a low to medium heat and fry the sandwiches for 2 minutes on each side until golden and the chocolate has melted inside.

3 Meanwhile, mix together the sugar and cinnamon in a bowl. Cut the chocolate croque-monsieurs in half diagonally, dust with cinnamon sugar, and serve.

Hot Waffles with Banana & Toffee-brandy Sauce

Toffee and bananas are a winning combination every time, but when used to top crispy golden waffles they will take you to another level.

SERVES 2

2 waffles
2 scoops vanilla ice cream
2 bananas, sliced
For the sauce
¼ cup/60ml heavy cream
1oz/25g molasses sugar
3 tbsp/45g butter
2 tbsp brandy

1 To make the sauce, place the cream, sugar, butter, and brandy in a small pan and heat gently until the sugar has dissolved. Turn up the heat and simmer for 3 minutes, or until thickened.

2 Warm the waffles in the microwave, or heat in the oven or toaster according to the instructions on the packet. Place a generous scoop of ice cream and half the sliced bananas on each one. Drizzle over the sauce and serve.

White Hot Chocolate
with Pink Marshmallows

There's something magical about white chocolate, and it's just fabulous in this sweet, moreish, frothy hot drink with melting marshmallows.

SERVES 2

2 cups/480ml whole milk
4oz/115g white chocolate
Pinch freshly grated nutmeg
Handful pink marshmallows

1 Heat the milk in a pan until boiling. Remove it from the heat and stir in the chocolate until melted.

2 Add the nutmeg to taste, and pour into two mugs. Scatter with plenty of marshmallows, and enjoy!

Two's Company

Dishes made for sharing

Figs with Buffalo Mozzarella & Prosciutto

Seek out the best buffalo mozzarella, choicest figs, and finest balsamic vinegar for this sumptuous dish. They will make the world of difference to the final flavor and are guaranteed to leave you with a rosy glow.

SERVES 2

1 (5oz/150g) packet buffalo mozzarella, torn into bitesize pieces
4 slices prosciutto
4 figs, halved
1 tbsp balsamic vinegar
2 tbsp extra virgin olive oil
Salt and freshly ground black pepper
Warmed ciabatta or focaccia, to serve

1 Arrange the mozzarella, prosciutto, and halved figs on a serving platter.

2 Drizzle balsamic vinegar and extra virgin olive oil over the top and season with salt and black pepper.

3 Serve with big chunks of warm ciabatta or focaccia for mopping up the dressing.

Vegetarian Antipasti
on Crisp Bruschetta

You can vary this recipe, making your own platter of antipasti, using deli-style jars of marinated vegetables and adding your own touches to make it feel special.

SERVES 2

4oz/115g fava beans
3oz/75g feta cheese
1 small garlic clove, crushed
1 tbsp lemon juice
5 tbsp extra virgin olive oil
8oz/225g roasted bell peppers
2 tbsp chopped black olives
1 tbsp capers
½ tbsp chopped fresh parsley
7oz/200g artichokes marinated in oil
Salt and freshly ground black pepper
For the bruschetta
6 slices baguette or ciabatta, cut
  ½in/1cm thick
1 garlic clove
2 tbsp extra virgin olive oil

1 Place the fava beans in a small pan of boiling water and simmer for 2 minutes. Drain and place in a food processor with the feta cheese, garlic, and lemon juice, and blend until smooth. Blend again, slowly drizzling in 4 tbsp oil until it is combined. Season with salt and freshly ground black pepper and transfer the mixture to a small bowl.

2 Toss the peppers with the remaining oil, olives, capers, and parsley, and transfer to another small bowl. Put the artichokes in a third bowl.

3 To make the bruschetta, place the bread on a baking sheet and toast on each side under the broiler. Rub with the garlic and drizzle with oil, and serve with the antipasti selection.

Baked Polenta Wedges
with Roasted Vegetables

A huge plate of these tasty morsels of polenta topped with lusciously indulgent toppings makes perfect snack food when you're curled up on the sofa watching a movie.

SERVES 2 GENEROUSLY

1lb 2oz/500g pack ready-made polenta
1 red bell pepper, deseeded and cut into eight pieces
3 tbsp extra virgin olive oil
4oz/115g mixed wild mushrooms
3 tbsp/45g butter
3oz/75g asparagus, trimmed
1 tbsp freshly grated Parmesan cheese
1 tbsp capers, drained
1 tbsp chopped fresh parsley
2 tbsp lemon juice
Salt and freshly ground black pepper

1 Preheat the oven to 400°F/200°C/Gas 6. Place the polenta at one end of a baking tray and the pepper pieces on the other. Drizzle with 1 tbsp of the oil and bake for 15 minutes.

2 Place the mushrooms in a small baking dish, dot over the butter, and season well. Add the asparagus to the baking tray with the pepper and polenta. Roast for a further 8–10 minutes, or until all the vegetables are tender and the polenta piping hot.

3 Cut the polenta into ½in/1cm slices and place on a large serving platter. Top one-third of the slices with asparagus, and scatter with the Parmesan. Scatter the second third with peppers, top with capers, and spoon the mushrooms over the remaining slices. Drizzle over the rest of the olive oil and scatter parsley on top. Squeeze over the lemon juice and serve while they're piping hot.

Eggplant Rolls Stuffed
with Pesto & Ricotta

**Utterly delicious, these big bites are
little morsels of loveliness. Serve with
a simple green salad and a glass of
chilled Pinot Grigio.**

MAKES 8

1 large eggplant, sliced ½in/1cm thick
    lengthways
2 tbsp olive oil
½ cup/125g ricotta cheese
2 tbsp pesto
½ cup/100g sunblush tomatoes, drained
    and chopped
1oz/25g wild arugula

1 Preheat the oven to 400°F/200°C/
Gas 6. Place the eggplant slices on a
baking sheet and brush both sides with
oil. Roast for 30 minutes, or until tender.
Allow them to cool slightly to make them
easier to handle.

2 Combine the ricotta, pesto, and
tomatoes and spread on to the eggplant
slices. Roll up and arrange on two serving
plates, with the join underneath. Scatter
over the arugula and serve.

Blue Cheese Fondue
with Pear & Walnut Bread

This fondue is a retro classic that has been given a thoroughly modern twist with a dash of citron vodka. Serve the accompaniments in three matching bowls lined up on a tray to give it a stunning and sleek modern look.

SERVES 2

4oz/115g Dolcelatte or Gorgonzola
  cheese, cubed
4oz/115g Mascarpone
1 tbsp citron vodka
2 pears, cored and cut into chunks
4 slices walnut bread, sliced into chunks
To serve
2oz/50g bag watercress or arugula
2 tbsp olive oil
Squeeze lemon juice

1 Place the cheeses in a small pan over a very low heat and stir until melted, then stir in the vodka.

2 Transfer the cheese mixture to a fondue pot and place on a burner at the table. Place the pear and bread on a serving platter or in individual bowls.

3 Mix the watercress or arugula with the oil and lemon juice, and serve with the fondue. Use fondue forks or skewers to dip the pear and bread into the fondue.

Chicken & Beef Satay
With Spicy Peanut Dip

Perfect for red-hot lovers, these spicy Indonesian skewers make a deliciously lazy feast as you lounge on the sofa. Enjoy as a substantial snack, or serve with salad for a light meal.

MAKES 16

½ tbsp red curry paste
3 tbsp coconut cream
Juice 1 lime
7oz/200g skinless chicken breast fillet, cut into strips
7oz/200g tender beef, cut into strips
For the sauce
1 tbsp Thai red curry paste
½ cup/120ml coconut cream
3 tbsp peanut butter
3 tbsp Thai fish sauce
1 tsp sugar
2 tbsp tamarind paste

1 Soak 16 wooden skewers in water for 20 minutes. Place the curry paste, coconut cream, and lime juice in a bowl and stir to mix. Add the meat and stir to coat. Marinate for at least 20 minutes.

2 Thread the meat in a zigzag manner on to the skewers, keeping the chicken and beef on separate skewers, and place on a baking sheet.

3 To make the sauce, place all the ingredients in a small pan and heat gently for 3–4 minutes, or until thick. Transfer to a serving bowl.

4 Meanwhile, broil the beef skewers for 1–2 minutes on each side and the chicken for 2–3 minutes on each side. Serve on a platter with the bowl of peanut sauce.

Vietnamese Roast Pork
in Lettuce Cups

If you're a fan of Peking duck and pancakes you'll love the idea of these little parcels. They're very hands on, so you'll have to keep your hands off each other (for a while!).

SERVES 2 AS A MAIN COURSE

12oz/350g pork tenderloin
2 tbsp char siu or any Asian
   barbecue sauce
To serve
½ cup/20g chopped fresh cilantro
½ cup/100g deseeded and finely
   chopped cucumber
½ mango, peeled, stoned, and chopped
Juice 1 lime
½ cup/120ml sweet chili sauce
leaves from 1 small round lettuce

1 Toss the pork in the char siu sauce. Leave to marinate for 1–3 hours, if possible, or continue without marinating. Preheat the oven to 300°F/150°C/Gas 2.

2 Line a roasting tray with foil and place the pork on top. Cover with more foil and roast for 25 minutes. Remove the top layer of foil and roast for 10 minutes more, or until just moist in the center. Leave the tenderloin to rest for at least 5 minutes, then slice thinly.

3 Toss the cilantro with the cucumber, mango, lime, and sweet chili sauce and place in a serving bowl. To eat, take a lettuce leaf and fill with a couple of pork slices, some chopped cucumber, and mango. Roll up and eat with your hands.

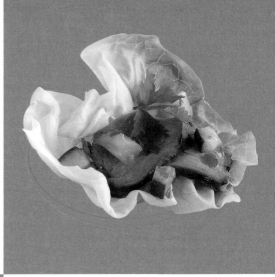

Spaghetti in Tomato Sauce,
Lady and the Tramp-style

Remember the movie The Lady and The Tramp when the two dogs eat the same strand of spaghetti and end up kissing? Well, we thought a simple pasta dish was a must for lovers. What's more, it's so simple to make that you'll have more time to spend with each other.

SERVES 2

3 tbsp/45g butter
12 basil leaves
1 garlic clove, sliced
1 (14oz/400g) can chopped plum tomatoes
7oz/200g spaghetti
2 tbsp aged balsamic vinegar
Freshly grated Parmesan cheese,
  to serve

1 Melt the butter in a skillet and add the basil and garlic. Fry for 2–3 minutes over a low heat until the garlic is golden. Add the tomatoes, turn the heat up to medium, and simmer for 15 minutes, or until thick.

2 Meanwhile, cook the pasta in a large pan of boiling salted water until al dente. Drain and return to the pan with the butter. Stir over a low heat until melted and add the balsamic vinegar. Turn up the heat, stir in the vinegar, and then add the tomato sauce. Serve sprinkled with Parmesan cheese.

Spanish Meatballs

in Tomato & Paprika Sauce

Try making these meatballs with veal—they're tender and full of flavor. The smoky sweet sauce just begs to be mopped up with wedges of crusty bread.

SERVES 2

12oz/350g ground veal or beef
3oz/75g breadcrumbs soaked
  in 2 tbsp milk
3 garlic cloves, crushed
½ tsp crushed chili
2 tbsp chopped fresh parsley
1 small onion, chopped
2 tbsp olive oil
1 tsp smoked paprika
1 tbsp tomato paste
1 (12oz/350g) can chopped plum
  tomatoes
5 tbsp red wine
½ tsp dried oregano
Salt and freshly ground black pepper
Crusty bread, to serve

1 Preheat the oven to 425°F/220°C/Gas 7. Place the ground meat in a mixing bowl with the soaked breadcrumbs, one clove of crushed garlic, and the chili, and mix together using your hands. Season generously and roll into ten walnut-size balls. Place on a baking sheet, and bake for 15–20 minutes, or until lightly golden.

2 Meanwhile cook the onion in a skillet with the oil for 6–7 minutes, or until soft. Add the remaining garlic and paprika, and cook for a further 2 minutes. Stir in the tomato paste, tomatoes, red wine, and oregano. Simmer uncovered for about 10 minutes, or until thick.

3 Serve the meatballs with the sauce and plenty of bread to mop up the juices.

Chilled Oysters with Hot & Spicy Chorizo Sausage

Swallow an icy-cold briny oyster and then follow it with a slice of hot, spicy chorizo sausage—it's a match made in heaven. Spicy chili stimulates certain areas of the brain, and oysters are reputed to have potent aphrodisiac properties—so the combination is sure stimulate your romantic side.

SERVES 2

12 oysters
4oz/115g chunky chorizo sausage, sliced
Tabasco sauce and lemon wedges,
  to serve

1 Open the oysters by wrapping your hand in a dishtowel and holding the oyster flat side up in the wrapped hand. Slide an oyster knife or small, flat-headed screwdriver into the hinge end and move it back and forth gently, pressing it further in to prize the shell open.

2 Once the shell releases, scrape a knife across the flat side of the shell to release the oyster. Remove and discard the top shell and serve the oyster in the other half. Repeat with the remaining oysters and arrange on a serving platter.

3 Heat a skillet over a low heat and fry the chorizo for 30 seconds on each side until crisp. Transfer to a small bowl and serve with the oysters.

Seafood Platter with Garlic & Tarragon Mayonnaise

A simple but luxurious dish that you can quickly throw together to make someone feel completely spoilt. Buy the crab already dressed to save time.

SERVES 2

4 scallops, cooked
4oz/115g cooked peeled jumbo shrimp
1 dressed crab, about 10½oz/300g
1 lobster, about 1½lb/700g, cooked and
  split in half

For the tarragon mayonnaise
4 tbsp mayonnaise
1 garlic clove, crushed
2 tbsp finely chopped fresh tarragon
2 tbsp lemon juice
Salt and freshly ground black pepper

1 To make the tarragon mayonnaise, place the mayonnaise, garlic, tarragon, and lemon juice in a small bowl and season with salt and pepper. Mix well.

2 Arrange the different shellfish on a large serving platter and serve with the tarragon mayonnaise for dipping.

Mussels with Chili & Sweet Basil

Cook these fabulous mussels when they are in season as you need good, juicy mussels to match the big flavors of this spicy, fragrant dish.

SERVES 2

1 tbsp sunflower oil
3 garlic cloves, crushed
6 green onions, roughly chopped
1 large green chili, chopped
2¼lb/1kg mussels, cleaned and beards removed
1 tbsp sugar
1 tbsp Thai fish sauce
1 tbsp Thai green curry paste
1 cup/240ml chicken stock
1 cup/20g fresh Thai basil leaves

1 Heat a wok or large pan over a high heat until smoking. Add the oil, garlic, half the green onions, the chili, and mussels. Stir-fry for 2 minutes, or until the shells are open, discarding any shells that remain closed.

2 Stir in the remaining ingredients except the basil leaves, and simmer for a further 2 minutes. Scatter with the fresh basil leaves and the remaining green onions, and serve.

Dinner à Deux

Seductive suppers for luxurious lovers

Carpaccio of Beef
with Arugula & Goat's Cheese

There's nothing more delicious than a good piece of fillet steak, and this is a fine way of making sure it is cooked to perfection. The tangy lemon juice really helps to bring out all the flavors and stimulate your taste buds.

SERVES 2

2 tbsp extra virgin olive oil
9oz/250g fillet of beef
1oz/25g wild arugula
2oz/50g crumbly goat's cheese
2 tbsp lemon juice
Freshly ground black pepper

1 Heat a skillet over a high heat until smoking. Add ½ tbsp of the oil and then the beef. Sear on all sides for 1 minute, or until lightly golden on the outside but still raw in the middle.

2 Leave the beef to rest for 5 minutes, then slice it as thinly as you can and arrange on a serving plate.

3 Scatter the arugula over the beef, then crumble over the goat's cheese. Drizzle with the remaining oil and sprinkle with lemon juice. Season with freshly ground black pepper, and serve.

Watermelon & Feta Salad
with Fresh Mint

Wait until watermelon is in season and at its most sweet and juicy before making this salad, so that you can taste the contrast between the sweet melon and the salty feta cheese. The fresh mint leaves add a wonderful dimension to the flavour of the salad.

SERVES 2

½ small watermelon, cut into cubes
1 cup/200g feta cheese
8 mint leaves
3 tbsp olive oil
Salt and freshly ground black pepper

1 Place the cubes of watermelon on a serving plate and crumble over the feta.

2 Chop the mint and add to the olive oil. Season with salt and freshly ground black pepper, and pour over the salad. Serve.

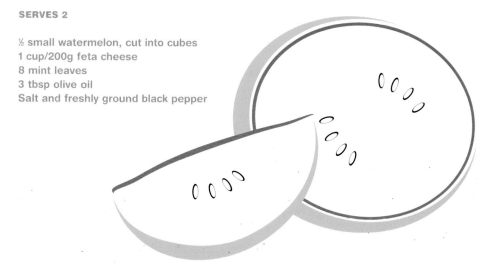

Tabouleh with Cucumber Hearts & Hot Smoked Salmon

Hot smoked salmon is more like smoked mackerel or trout than regular smoked salmon—and these fish make a great alternative. You don't have to cut the cucumber into hearts but it adds an affectionate touch to the dish, when you notice one nestled in amongst the grains.

SERVES 2

½ cup/100g bulgur wheat
½ cucumber, sliced ½in/1cm thick
4oz/115g baby plum tomatoes, halved
5oz/150g hot smoked salmon, flaked
  into chunks
3 tbsp olive oil
Juice ½ lemon
1 cup/30g chopped flat leaf parsley
½ cup/15g chopped mint
Salt and freshly ground black pepper

1 Place the bulgur wheat in a pan with cold water, bring to the boil, and simmer for 15 minutes, or until tender. Drain well in a sieve, pressing out all the water.

2 Using a heart-shaped cookie cutter, cut the cucumber slices into chunky hearts. Add to the bulgur wheat with the tomatoes and salmon. Stir in the oil, lemon juice, parsley, and mint, and season to taste. Serve.

Butternut Squash & Goat's Cheese Cannelloni

Sweet, earthy squash and creamy goat's cheese go fantastically well together. Tease your taste buds with this hearty cannelloni dish, which is smothered in a nutty sage butter.

SERVES 2

1 small butternut squash, halved
  and deseeded
2 egg yolks
3 tbsp milk
5oz/150g goat's cheese
6 sheets fresh lasagne
3 tbsp/45g butter
2 tbsp pine nuts
1 tbsp chopped fresh sage
Salt and freshly ground black pepper

1 Preheat the oven to 425°F/220°C/ Gas 7. Wrap the squash in foil and roast for 1 hour, or until soft. Allow to cool, and then scoop out the flesh and place in a mixing bowl with the egg yolks, milk, goat's cheese, and plenty of seasoning. Mix thoroughly and set aside.

2 Meanwhile, cook the lasagne in a pan of boiling water for 3–4 minutes, or until tender, then drain and refresh under cold running water.

3 Place 2 tbsp of the squash in each lasagne sheet and roll up from the shortest end. Place in a buttered baking dish and dot over the butter. Sprinkle over the pine nuts and sage and return to the oven for 5–6 minutes, or until the butter is lightly golden. Serve.

Spicy Lemon Grass Tofu
with Asparagus & Baby Corn

Heat things up a bit with this spicy, aromatic stir-fry, full of nourishing flavors and vegetables for vitality.

SERVES 2

1 tbsp oil
1 large red chili, chopped
1 lemon grass stalk, ground finely
3 kaffir lime leaves, chopped
1 garlic clove, crushed
3 slices fresh root ginger
1 tbsp tamarind paste
1 tbsp soy sauce
1 tbsp honey
13oz/375g firm tofu, cut into cubes
6 baby corn
12 asparagus tips

1 Heat a wok or skillet over a medium-high heat and add the oil. Add the chili, lemon grass, lime leaves, garlic, and ginger and stir-fry for 1 minute.

2 Add the tamarind, soy sauce, and honey. Toss in the tofu, baby corn, asparagus, and 4 tbsp water, and simmer for 2–3 minutes, or until the vegetables are tender. Serve immediately.

Thai Scallops with Ginger, Lime & Chili Butter

If you can, buy big, fresh scallops that are still in their shells. The flavors are fragrant, spicy, and tart—making it the perfect dish for lovers.

SERVES 2

6 king scallops, cleaned and returned
  to their cleaned half-shells
3 sprigs fresh cilantro
For the butter
3 tbsp/45g butter
1 red chili, finely chopped
1 tsp fresh ginger, peeled and grated
1 garlic clove, crushed
Juice and rind of ½ lime
1 tbsp Thai fish sauce
1 tsp sugar

1 To make the spicy butter, place the ingredients in a small pan and heat until the butter has melted and the sugar has dissolved completely.

2 Spoon the butter over the raw scallops in their shells and place on a baking sheet. Place under a preheated broiler and cook for 4 minutes. Serve topped with fresh cilantro.

> **Cook's Tip**
>
> If you cannot find scallops still in their shells, pan fry them in ½ tbsp oil for 1 minute each side and then drizzle the warm butter over the top.

Seared Tuna Steaks

with Cucumber & Ginger Salad

For a light supper that is packed with taste, this tuna dish will hit the mark. The fresh Asian flavors used here go particularly well with the meaty fish.

SERVES 2

4 tbsp olive oil
Juice ½ lime
1 tsp grated fresh root ginger
½ cup/10g fresh small mint leaves
½ cup/10g fresh cilantro leaves
1 cucumber, peeled, seeded, and sliced
9oz/250g fresh tuna steak, about
  1in/2.5cm thick
Salt

1 Place 3½ tbsp of the oil with the lime juice, ginger, and herbs in a bowl, and mix well. Add the cucumber and season with salt. Set aside at room temperature.

2 Heat a skillet over a high heat until smoking, and add the remaining oil. Sear the tuna for 1 minute on each side and then slice thinly.

3 Arrange on serving plates, top with the cucumber salad, and serve immediately.

Monkfish Saltimbocca
with Truffle Paste & Prosciutto

Sweet, firm monkfish is the perfect choice for lovers. It tastes divine and has such a special flavor it always feels like an indulgent treat.

SERVES 2

5 large slices prosciutto
2 × 12oz/350g monkfish tail fillets (one tail with the bone removed)
2 tbsp truffle paste or tapenade
2 tbsp pine nuts
1 tbsp olive oil
Juice 1 lemon
Steamed small green beans, to serve

1 Preheat the oven to 400°F/200°C/ Gas 6. Lay the prosciutto on a chopping board so that it overlaps, and place the monkfish on top. Spread the truffle paste or tapenade all over the fish and wrap it up in the prosciutto.

2 Transfer to a baking dish and scatter the pine nuts evenly over the top. Drizzle over the oil and roast for 15–20 minutes, or until firm and cooked through. Sprinkle over the lemon juice and serve with steamed green beans.

Lobster Tails

with Champagne & Chive Risotto

You can use crayfish, large shrimp, or even live lobster for this dish. If you prefer to use live lobster, drop it into boiling water and simmer for 8 minutes, and then split and broil as described.

SERVES 2

3 tbsp/45g butter, plus extra for brushing
3 shallots, chopped
¼ cup/75g arborio or vialone nano rice
1 cup/240ml champagne
2 cups/480ml simmering fish stock
1 cooked lobster tail, split in half
3 tbsp heavy cream
3 tbsp chopped chives
1 oz/25g freshly grated Parmesan cheese
Salt and freshly ground black pepper

1 Melt the butter in a pan and sauté the shallots gently for about 5 minutes, or until softening. Add the rice and cook for 1 minute, stirring.

2 Pour in the champagne and stir until evaporated. Add ¾ cup/180ml of the simmering stock and stir until evaporated. Repeat with the remaining stock until the rice is tender.

3 Meanwhile, brush the lobster with butter and place on a baking sheet. Place under a medium broiler for 2 minutes, or until warmed through.

4 Stir the cream into the rice and add the chives and Parmesan cheese. Season to taste with salt and pepper and spoon on to two plates. Top each portion with a halved lobster tail and serve immediately.

Stir-fried Chicken
with Chili & Sweet Basil

Sweet basil is said to be an aphrodisiac. It is warming and spicy with a slight aniseed taste. Sweet basil is much more aromatic than regular basil but if you can't get it try cilantro instead.

SERVES 2

1 tbsp vegetable oil
2 chicken breast fillets, sliced thinly
2 garlic cloves, crushed
2 large red chilies, deseeded, and sliced
½ onion, cut into 1¼in/3cm chunks
3 tbsp Thai fish sauce
1 tbsp dark soy sauce
1 tbsp brown sugar
1 cup/20g sweet basil leaves
Steamed rice, to serve

1 Heat a wok over a high heat until smoking. Add the oil and then the chicken, garlic, and chilies. Stir-fry for 1 minute, and then add the onion. Continue stir-frying for 5 minutes, or until the chicken is cooked through.

2 Pour in the fish sauce and soy sauce, and sprinkle over the sugar. Bring to the boil and scatter with sweet basil. Serve immediately with steamed rice.

Duck with Berry Sauce

Moist duck breasts are always a treat, and taste fabulous topped with this robust, fruity sauce. It's such an easy dish to prepare, and looks incredibly sophisticated for a special meal.

SERVES 2

2 duck breasts
½ tsp salt
Pan-fried spinach, to serve
For the sauce
1 garlic clove, crushed
4 tbsp red wine
3 tbsp crème de cassis
¼ cup/60ml beef stock
1 tsp arrowroot mixed with 1 tbsp
   cold water
4oz/115g mixed berries, such as
   raspberries, blueberries, blackcurrants,
   and blackberries

1 Score the skin of the duck five or six times, being careful not to cut into the flesh. Rub the skin with salt. Heat a skillet over a medium heat and place the duck in the pan, skin side down, and cook for 10 minutes.

2 Pour away the fat from the pan, turn over the duck, and cook for 3–4 minutes. Remove from the pan and leave to rest while you make the sauce.

3 Add the garlic to the pan and stir for 30 seconds, then add the wine, crème de cassis, and stock. Simmer vigorously for 3 minutes. Stir in the arrowroot mixture and return to the boil. Stir in the berries.

4 Slice the duck and arrange on two serving plates. Drizzle over the sauce and serve with pan-fried spinach.

Quail with Pomegranate Sauce & Filbert Couscous

Knock them dead with his beautiful
and impressive dish. Look out for
pomegranate molasses in ethnic stores.

SERVES 2

1 tbsp olive oil
1 tbsp/15g butter
4 quails, halved
1 garlic clove, crushed
½ cup/120ml white wine
2 tsp pomegranate molasses
½ pomegranate, seeds removed
For the couscous
3oz/75g couscous
½ cup/120ml boiling water
1 tbsp filbert-nut oil
1oz/25g filberts, chopped and toasted
1 tsp dried mint
3 tbsp chopped fresh parsley
3oz/75g dried cherries or cranberries

1 Heat the oil and butter in a large
flameproof casserole and brown the
quails for 5 minutes, or until golden all
over. Add the garlic to the pan and cook
for 30 seconds, then pour in the wine,
pomegranate molasses, and pomegranate
seeds. Cover and cook over medium heat
for 15 minutes, or until the quails are
cooked through.

2 Meanwhile, put the couscous in a
mixing bowl and pour over the water. Set
aside for 5 minutes to allow the grains
to swell. Stir in the oil, nuts, herbs, and
dried fruit. Pile the couscous on to two
plates and serve the quails on top.

> **Cook's Tip**
>
> To remove the seeds from the
> pomegranate, halve the fruit and then
> turn it upside down and bang on the back
> of the shell with a wooden rolling pin.

5

Sweet Nothings
Desserts to indulge your wicked side

Sweet and Nutty Caramel Strawberries

These strawberries make a lovely little nibble after dinner, or you can use them to decorate a cake or dessert. They will even make a bowl of plain old vanilla ice cream look amazing!

MAKES 24

1 cup/225g granulated sugar
3 tbsp water
1lb/450g strawberries
3 tbsp chopped, toasted filberts

1 Place the sugar and water in a clean pan and heat gently until all the sugar has dissolved. Increase the heat and simmer for 6–10 minutes, or until golden. Take off the heat just before the caramel turns golden. If the caramel becomes too dark or smells burnt, plunge the base of the pan into a bowl of cold water to cool it down—being careful not to get any water into the caramel.

2 Take half the strawberries and, holding the strawberry by the stalk, dip the lower half of each one in the caramel. Set on a baking sheet lined with waxed paper and leave to harden. If the caramel in the pan hardens, return it to a very low heat and swirl it around until it softens.

3 Take the remaining strawberries, and dip the lower half in the caramel as before, then roll in the chopped nuts. Leave to harden.

Chocolate Truffles
with Orange Flower Water

**These bitesize mouthfuls of melting
white chocolate truffle are perfect
for tempting each other with. They're
particularly good served with a glass
of sparkling champagne.**

MAKES 10

⅓ cup/80ml heavy cream
5oz/150g white cooking chocolate
1–2 tbsp orange flower water
4 tbsp unsweetened cocoa powder

1 Heat the cream in a small pan until
almost boiling. Take off the heat, leave to
cool for 5 minutes, or until warm enough
to touch, and then stir in the chocolate
and orange flower water until smooth.

2 Dust your hands in a little cocoa and
place the remainder on a flat plate. Scoop
out a walnut-size piece of chocolate with
a spoon and roll it in your hands. Roll in
cocoa and place on a clean plate. Repeat
with the remaining mixture. Chill for an
hour to firm up.

Loveheart Cupcakes
with Raspberry Filling

Make these all-in-one cupcakes on a dreary, rainy afternoon and they will instantly cheer you both up.

MAKES 12

½ cup/120g sweet butter, softened
½ cup/120g superfine sugar
2 eggs, beaten
1 cup/120g self-rising flour
½ tsp vanilla extract
2 tbsp milk
For the filling
½ cup/100g Mascarpone cheese
2 tbsp milk
2 tbsp confectioner's sugar
½ cup/75g raspberries
1 tbsp confectioner's sugar, for dusting

1 Place the butter, sugar, eggs, and flour in a bowl and add the vanilla extract and milk. Blend together using an electric mixer until thoroughly mixed.

2 Fill a 12-hole cupcake pan with paper cases, and spoon a heaped tablespoon of the mixture into each one. Bake for 18 minutes, or until a skewer comes out clean, then leave to cool completely.

3 To make the filling, mix together the Mascarpone, milk, and sugar, beating out any lumps until well blended. Add half the raspberries and crush slightly as you stir them in.

4 Using a knife, cut out a large, deep round from each cup cake, about 1¼in/3cm wide, and cut off the spongy center. Cut the tops into heart shapes. Spoon the filling into the holes and top with the hearts. Decorate the plate with extra raspberries and dust lightly with confectioner's sugar before serving.

Rose-scented Panna Cotta

These delicate 'cooked creams' are flavored with rose water—the flavoring that gives Turkish delight its unique and distinctive taste. Decorate the creams with a few fresh pink rose petals for that really romantic touch.

SERVES 2

2 leaves gelatin
3 tbsp milk
2 cups/480ml whipping cream
2 tbsp superfine sugar
1 tbsp rose water
Fresh rose petals, to decorate

1 Soak the gelatin in the milk until soft. Place the cream, sugar, and rose water in a small pan and heat gently until almost boiling. Take off the heat and allow to cool. Add the milk from the gelatin and, once cooled, add the gelatin itself. Stir until completely dissolved.

2 Pour the mixture into two ¾ cup/180ml dariole moulds or pudding basins. Cover and refrigerate overnight. Unmould and serve decorated with rose petals.

Turkish Delight Ice Cream
with Moroccan Mint Tea

Enjoy this luscious combination of hot tea and exotic rose water-flavored ice cream—to heat things up, or cool things down, depending on the moment! Look out for authentic Turkish delight, rather than the artificially flavoured variety.

SERVES 2

1 tbsp rosewater
1 cup/240ml tub good quality vanilla ice cream, slightly softened
4oz/115g Turkish Delight, chopped
2 sprigs mint
3 tbsp sugar
2 cups/500ml boiling water

1 Pour the rose water over the ice cream and scatter the Turkish Delight on top. Stir until combined. Place back in the freezer for 30 minutes, or until the ice cream has firmed up again. Scoop into two serving bowls.

2 To make the tea, grind the mint with the sugar in a heatproof pitcher until the mint has broken up a little. Pour over the boiling water and leave to stand for about 5 minutes. Pour the tea into two cups and serve with the ice cream.

Muscat-poached Grapes
with Thick and Creamy Yogurt

When simplicity calls, try this moreish dessert out for size. The grapes become almost perfumed and all they need is a dollop of velvety smooth yogurt to really enhance their flavor.

SERVES 2

4oz/115g black seedless grapes
1 cup/240ml muscat dessert wine
2 tbsp honey
1 vanilla bean, split lengthways
1 cup/240ml strained plain yogurt

1 Place the grapes, wine, honey, and vanilla in a pan and simmer for 5 minutes, or until the grapes have softened. Lift out the grapes using a slotted spoon and transfer them to a bowl.

2 Turn up the heat and boil the syrup for 10 minutes, or until thick. Divide the yogurt between two serving glasses and top with the grapes and their syrup.

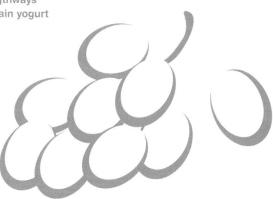

Chewy Meringues with Orange-scented Mascarpone

Fluffy, pure-white meringues are sensational filled with zesty orange cream and topped with pink, jewel-colored pomegranate seeds.

MAKES 2

3 egg whites
⅔ cup/150g superfine sugar
½ tsp white wine vinegar
1 heaped tsp cornstarch
For the topping
½ cup/100g Mascarpone
3 tbsp orange juice
Rind of 1 orange
½ pomegranate

1 Preheat the oven to 275°F/140°C/Gas 1. Place the egg whites in a bowl and beat them until stiff, using an electric hand beater. Add ⅓ cup/75g of the sugar, a tablespoonful at a time, beating after each addition until glossy. Add the remaining sugar and beat gently. Mix the vinegar and cornstarch together in a small bowl and stir into the mixture.

2 Spoon the mixture on to waxed paper to make two 4in/10cm circles. Bake for 1 hour, then leave to cool.

3 Meanwhile, mix the Mascarpone, orange juice, and rind together. Bash the back of the pomegranate with a rolling pin to remove the seeds. Top the meringues with the Mascarpone mixture and scatter the pomegranate seeds on top. Serve immediately.

Champagne Jelly
with Blackcurrants

This is definitely a jelly for grown ups only. The champagne flavor is subtle and elegant, and the whole experience thoroughly pleasurable.

SERVES 2

½ cup/120g superfine sugar
½ cup/180ml water
½ cup/180ml champagne
3 sheets gelatin, soaked in 4 tbsp water
Blackcurrants and light cream, to serve

1 Place the sugar and water in a small pan over a low heat and stir until dissolved. Turn up the heat and boil for about 5 minutes, or until syrupy.

2 Take off the heat and add just enough of the champagne to cool the syrup slightly. (The mixture must be hot enough to melt the gelatin but cool enough not to cook it.) Beat in the soaked gelatin, until it has completely dissolved, and then pour in the remaining champagne.

3 Pour the mixture into two ¾ cup/180ml moulds or one 1½ cup/350ml mould, and place in the refrigerator to set. Unmould by inverting on to a plate and giving the mould a short, sharp shake. Serve with fresh blackcurrants and cream.

Fresh Figs Baked
with Almond Butter

There's something immensely sexy about figs—and you can't beat this recipe with its nutty, crispy topping and the warm, juicy figs underneath.

SERVES 2

4 heaped tbsp Mascarpone
1 tbsp amaretto liqueur
4 plump figs, halved
2 tbsp superfine sugar
1oz/25g sweet butter, softened
1oz/25g ground almonds
Pinch freshly grated nutmeg

1 Mix together the Mascarpone and amaretto liqueur until smooth. Set aside.

2 Preheat the broiler. Place the figs cut side up on a baking tray lined with waxed paper. Broil for 2 minutes, or until the flesh is softened.

3 Cream together the sugar, butter, and almonds. Place a spoonful on each fig half and broil for 1–2 minutes, keeping a careful eye on them, because they will burn quite quickly.

4 Serve the hot figs straight away with a spoonful of the flavored Mascarpone.

Strawberries in Pimms Syrup with Shortbread

Perfect for a romantic summer picnic or after a barbecue lunch in the garden, there is hardly any preparation needed for this delightful dessert.

SERVES 2

½ cup/120ml Pimms
½ cup/120ml orange juice
2 tbsp superfine sugar
2 sprigs mint
2 cups/200g strawberries, hulled and halved
4 shortbread cookies, to serve

1 Place the Pimms, orange juice, sugar, and mint in a mixing bowl. Add the strawberries and leave them to macerate at room temperature for 30 minutes.

2 Serve the strawberries and juices in small bowls with the shortbread cookies.

Chocolate Rum Fondue
with Fresh Fruit Dippers

Chocolate fondue is always the ultimate indulgence. Just keep dipping until you run out of fruit ... then use a spoon or your fingers to scrape up the rest!

SERVES 2

3oz/75g bittersweet chocolate,
  broken up
3 tbsp heavy cream
1 tbsp/15g butter
2 tbsp water
1 tbsp rum
To dip
Pineapple chunks
Strawberries, halved
Marshmallows
Banana chunks

1 Place the chocolate, cream, butter, water, and rum in a heatproof bowl set over a pan of simmering water. Stir until the chocolate has melted and the mixture is smooth and creamy.

2 Take off the heat, pour the mixture into a fondue pot, and place on a burner at the table. Serve the fondue with the fruits and marshmallows, using fondue forks or wooden skewers to dip them into the sauce.

White & Dark Chocolate Cheesecake with Raspberries

With a creamy soft texture and delicious chocolate flavor, these cute little cheesecakes will leave you begging for just one more!

SERVES 2

3oz/75g Graham crackers, crushed
3 tbsp/45g sweet butter, melted
1 tbsp unsweetened cocoa powder

For the filling
3oz/75g white chocolate
3oz/75g full-fat cream cheese
6 tbsp crème fraîche or sour cream
2 tbsp confectioner's sugar

To decorate
3oz/75g raspberries
1oz/25g dark chocolate curls or grated dark chocolate
1 tbsp unsweetened cocoa powder

1 Mix together the Graham crackers, butter, and cocoa. Use two 3¼in/8cm round cookie cutters to shape the base. Place the cutters on a flat plate and divide the crackers between each of them. Press down on the crackers until firmly packed. Alternatively, you can line the base of two large ramekins with the cracker base. Place in the refrigerator to chill while you make the filling.

2 Melt the chocolate in a bowl over a pan of hot water. Beat together all the ingredients for the filling and pour on top of the bases. Chill for 2 hours, or until firm. Lift off the cookie cutters, top with raspberries, chocolate curls or grated chocolate, and dust with cocoa.

Weights and measures

The following conversions and equivalents will provide useful guidelines for international readers to follow. There's just one golden rule to remember when you're preparing your ingredients: always stay with one system of measurement—that way you'll achieve the best results from these recipes.

Liquid ingredients

½ tsp	=	2.5ml
1 tsp	=	5ml
1 tbsp.	=	15ml
2 tbsp	=	30ml
3 tbsp	=	45ml
¼ cup	=	60ml
⅓ cup	=	80ml
½ cup	=	125ml
⅔ cup	=	160ml
¾ cup	=	180ml
1 cup	=	250ml
1½ cups	=	375ml
2 cups	=	500ml
3 cups	=	750ml
4 cups	=	1 liter
5 cups	=	1.2 liters
6 cups	=	1.5 liters
8 cups	=	2 liters

Dry ingredients

¼oz	=	10g
½oz	=	15g
¾oz	=	20g
1oz	=	25g
1½oz	=	40g
2oz	=	50g
2½oz	=	65g
3oz	=	75g
3½oz	=	90g
4oz	=	115g
4½oz	=	130g
5oz	=	150g
6oz	=	175g
7oz	=	200g
8oz	=	225g

Measurements

1in	=	2.5cm

Glossary

The following culinary terms will provide useful guidelines for international readers to follow.

all-purpose flour: plain flour
arugula: rocket
bacon strips: bacon rashers
beet: beetroot
bell pepper: pepper
bittersweet chocolate: plain chocolate
broil: to grill
broiler: the grill
brown sugar: light muscovado sugar
cilantro: coriander
confectioner's sugar: icing sugar
cornstarch: cornflour
eggplant: aubergine
fatty bacon: streaky bacon
fava beans: broad beans
filberts: hazelnuts
Graham crackers: digestive biscuits

green onion: spring onion
ground: minced
heavy cream: double cream
light cream: single cream
molasses sugar: dark muscovado sugar
pitted: stoned
red bell pepper: red pepper
self-rising flour: self-raising flour
skillet: frying pan
slithered almonds: flaked almonds
strained plain yogurt: Greek yogurt
superfine sugar: caster sugar
sweet butter: unsalted butter
tomato paste: tomato purée
turbinado sugar: demerara sugar
vanilla bean: vanilla pod

Index

corn: spicy lemon grass tofu with asparagus and baby corn 75

Cosmopolitan 13

couscous: quail with pomegranate sauce and filbert couscous 87

crab: sexy sushi hand rolls 21

cranberry juice: Cosmopolitan 13

cream: rose-scented panna cotta 95

cucumber: seared tuna steaks with cucumber and ginger salad 78

tabouleh with cucumber hearts and hot smoked salmon 72

drinks: cocktails 10–17

white hot chocolate 46

duck with berry sauce 84

duck eggs with asparagus and chorizo dippers 31

eggplant rolls stuffed with pesto and ricotta 55

eggs: creamy scrambled eggs 34

soft boiled duck eggs with asparagus and chorizo dippers 31

fava beans: vegetarian antipasti 52

figs: figs with buffalo mozzarella and prosciutto 50

fresh figs baked with almond butter 103

fondues: blue cheese 56

chocolate rum 105

French toast with passion fruit and vanilla syrup 37

fruit dippers, chocolate rum fondue with 105

grapes, muscat-poached 97

halloumi drizzled with mint and chili oil 24

ham: roasted asparagus tips with lemon aioli 22

honey-roasted nuts 25

ice cream: hot waffles with banana and toffee-brandy sauce 45

Turkish delight ice cream 96

jelly, champagne 100

limes: mango and lime Caipirinha 10

little devil, 10

lobster tails with champagne and chive risotto 80

loveheart cupcakes 92

mango and lime Caipirinha 10

marshmallows, white hot chocolate with 46

meatballs in tomato and paprika sauce 62

meringues with orange-scented mascarpone 99

mint tea, Moroccan 96

monkfish saltimbocca 79

Moroccan mint tea 96

muscat-poached grapes 97

mussels with chili and sweet basil 67

nori seaweed: sexy sushi hand rolls 21

nuts, honey-roasted 25

oysters: chilled oysters with hot and spicy chorizo sausage 63

oysters with shallot and red wine vinaigrette 18

pancakes, blueberry 39

panna cotta, rose-scented 95

passion fruit, French toast with vanilla syrup and 37

pastries, sweet sticky plum and almond 42

peaches: sweet sticky peach and almond pastries 42

white peach Bellini 12

pear and walnut bread, blue cheese fondue with 56

peppers: vegetarian antipasti 52

pesto, eggplant rolls stuffed with ricotta and 55

Pimms syrup, strawberries in 104

plum and almond pastries 42

polenta wedges with roasted vegetables 53